Christians often take
They point out, with
son like shallow mate.....
at this because Christ is reduced to a soundbite or a pawn in a cultural
war. The devil smirks because the sinner is left with law upon law.
What the sinner actually needs is what Morales and Jones provide in
this devotional, Christ. Christ in a manger. Christ on the cross. Christ
on the page. Christ in ears. Christ for the sinner. Christ for you.

—Rev. Dr. Michael Berg
Assistant Professor of Theology Wisconsin Lutheran College

My sinful nature thinks this is a terrible devotional because it doesn't
point me to myself. Every devotion is centered on Jesus and only Him
and His work to save us! The saint in me, however, loves this devotional for that same reason! There's no fluff: just all Jesus and His
work for us, lovingly portrayed against the backdrop of the Advent
and Christmas seasons. I'll be recommending it to the congregation
I serve for sure!

—Pastor Mark Buetow
Zion Lutheran Church and School McHenry, Illinois

The Sinner/Saint Devotional: Advent and Christmas is a journey of slow
steps in a pivotal season of hope and anticipation. Amidst the hustle
and bustle of the busiest time of the year, I recommend this devotional
as a guide to pause and reflect on the good things that have happened,
and a reminder that the best is still to come.

—Steve Veasey, Illustrator and author of *Thin Spaces*

"Kathy and Kyle have given us a gift. This devotional is a beautiful
invitation to slow down and be present during the final chaotic weeks
of another year. These pages help us to wait with hope as we digest the
slowness of God and the quick love He has for us. I cannot recommend
this enough."

—Tanner Olson, Founder, Written to Speak

Oftentimes, the contemporary Christian knows little about Advent and the ultimate goal of Christmas. Many see the season as a time to reflect on what Jesus did long ago or to consume. Journey with Kathy Morales and Kyle G. Jones as they masterfully walk you through the Christian calendar for four weeks of Advent and then Christmas. Showing how Christ is for you. Uniquely. Particularly. Continuously.

—FLAME, Grammy Nominated Christian Rap Artist

Advent is a season of preparation and longing. We are preparing to celebrate the festival of our Lord's birth at Christmas while longing for Him to return and make all things new. During these times our God is faithful and sustains us with His promises. Knowing that it is only these promises that will keep us along the way, Kathy and Kyle have given us a gift with this wonderful devotional. Each devotion helps carry us through this season of waiting by placarding Jesus before our eyes. As you work through this gospel-saturated book, you will daily and richly receive the gifts of hope and comfort because of God's faithfulness to His promises for you! This Sinner/Saint Devotional is truly a gift for us all this Advent and Christmas season!

—Pastor Bob Hiller (Senior Pastor of Community Lutheran Church Escondido/San Marcos, CA, co-host of White Horse Inn, and content editor for The Craft of Preaching)

— *The* —
SINNER / SAINT DEVOTIONAL: ADVENT & CHRISTMAS

— *The* —
SINNER / SAINT
ADVENT & CHRISTMAS
DEVOTIONAL

DEVOTIONS FOR ADVENT AND CHRISTMAS,
FOCUSED ON JESUS'S WORK FOR YOU

KYLE G. JONES & KATHRYN MORALES

Foreword by:
CHAD BIRD

The Sinner/Saint Devotional: Advent and Christmas

© 2022 New Reformation Publications

Published by
1517 Publishing
PO Box 54032
Irvine, CA 92619-4032

Publisher's Cataloging-in-Publication
(Provided by Cassidy Cataloguing Services, Inc.).

Names: Jones, Kyle G., author. | Morales, Kathryn, author. | Bird, Chad, writer of
            supplementary textual content.
Title:The sinner/saint devotional : Advent and Christmas / by Kyle G. Jones and
            Kathryn Morales ; foreword by Chad Bird.
Other titles: Sinner saint devotional : Advent and Christmas
Description: Irvine, CA : 1517 Publishing, [2022] | Series: The sinner/
            saint devotional series | Includes bibliographical references.
Identifiers: ISBN: 978-1-956658-00-2 (paperback) | 978-1-956658-01-9 (ebook)
Subjects: LCSH: Lutheran Church—Prayers and devotions. | Bible—Devotional use. |
            Advent—Prayers and devotions. | Christmas—Prayers and devotions. |
            Devotional exercises. | LCGFT: Devotional literature. | BISAC: RELIGION /
            Holidays / Christmas & Advent. | RELIGION / Holidays / General. |
            RELIGION / Christian Living / Devotional.
Classification: LCC: BX8067.C4 J66 2022 | DDC: 242/.33—dc23

Printed in the United States of America.

Cover art by Zachariah James Stuef.

To my husband, Ryan
—Kathy

To my wife, Lauren, and daughter, Elliot
—Kyle

Contents

THE THIRD WEEK OF ADVENT

THE FOURTH WEEK OF ADVENT

THE TWELVE DAYS OF CHRISTMAS

Foreword

The church seems to have everything backward in Advent. While the world is making a mad dash toward Christmas, pedal to the metal, the church coasts off the side of the highway, kills the engine, kicks her feet up on the dashboard, and gazes into the distant horizon with a smile playing at the corner of her lips. She sits. She waits. She muses. If for the world, December is a roaring race toward the 25th, then Advent is a sober embrace of how our God moseys about everywhere in grandma gear.

The Lord is in no hurry. Never has been. After he dropped the promise of a saving Seed into the laps of Adam and Eve, he made them and their descendants wait millennia for that Seed to be cooing in Mary's arms. When Israel was shackled by Egyptian chains, they waited, then waited some more, until finally the Lord sent an octogenarian named Moses to liberate them. And even when Jesus came along, he did not kickstart his ministry at the age of eighteen or twenty-five, but only after he had thirty years of life experience under his belt. The police will never hand our Lord a speeding ticket.

In Advent especially, we enter the timetable of our Lord. Though our spiritual home is in the new covenant, we share a tent with our Old Testament brothers and sisters. We reenter their lives, lives shaped by the hopeful expectation of the Messiah. The prophet like Moses. The Immanuel of Isaiah. We sit at the feet of the camel-skin-clad prophet in bad need of a haircut, with locust legs stuck between his teeth, preaching, "Repent!" as he baptizes sinners in the Jordan. We shout Hosanna as the Rabbi from Nazareth, a few days before Passover, rides the donkey-mobile over a carpet of palms into the city of his father, David. There he will assume a cruel Roman-made throne, crowned with the thorned fruit of Adam's rebellion.

So that we don't miss any of this, during Advent, let's sip not guzzle. Walk not sprint. As an aid to this exercise in countercultural backwardness, drink in the biblically-saturated meditations in this wonderful little book. Let their words roam free in the home of your mind, to confront you, console you, prompt you, and especially to bring you to Jesus and Jesus to you. Use the verses every day as a springboard for prayer and reflection. Read them alone. Read them to your family. Heck, read them to your Uber driver. You might just make his day.

Advent is, in my opinion, the most wonderful time of the year. A month pregnant with hope. A month that whispers, amidst the guffaws and blah-blah-shallowness of a loud and drunken world, "Psst. Listen, friend. Peace, joy, forgiveness, and life are yours in spades through the one whose singular calling in life is to love you and save you to the end."

A blessed Advent to you all. Jesus loves you.

CHAD BIRD

A note on the number of days in Advent and using this Devotional

Unlike the season of Lent, which has 40 days (not counting Sundays), the number of days in Advent changes every year. There can be between 22 and 28 days. The number of days depends on which day of the week Christmas Day falls.

The subtraction or addition of the number of days in Advent happens in the fourth week. This is because one of the requirements of the season of Advent is that it begins four Sundays before Christmas Day. So if December 25th falls on a Monday, then Christmas Eve is also on the Fourth Sunday of Advent. If Christmas Day falls on a Sunday, then the fourth week of Advent has seven days with Christmas Eve being on Saturday.

We wrote a devotion for every possible day of Advent. This way, you will have a devotion to read for every day of Advent during whatever year you use this devotional.

You may notice that there is no Saturday in the fourth week of Advent. We labeled it "Christmas Eve" since that is what it would be if there was a Saturday in the fourth week of Advent in a given year. The devotion for Christmas Eve can be read on whatever day Christmas Eve falls that year. Then, you skip the remaining devotions in the fourth week of Advent to read Christmas Day's devotion, followed by the devotions for the following 11 days of Christmas.

The FIRST WEEK *of* ADVENT

Walking Backward into Christmas

BLESSED BE THE LORD GOD OF ISRAEL, FOR HE HAS VISITED AND REDEEMED HIS PEOPLE AND HAS RAISED UP A HORN OF SALVATION FOR US IN THE HOUSE OF HIS SERVANT DAVID.

—Luke 1:68-69

Time has a hold on us. The lead-up to Christmas—what the church calls Advent—has a way of bringing time's grip on us into the foreground. Time moves us in one direction whether we're ready or not. But time's power is limited. It can't dictate the direction we face. We are free to face backward as it pulls us forward.

The season of Advent reverses our view to what has been as we move closer to what is to come. Evidence hangs on our Christmas trees. As we hang our ornaments—the 20-year-old childhood crafts, hand-me-downs from generations past, and gifts to mark special occasions—we pivot to face what has been as we move toward what will be. We prepare for the coming Christmas by looking back and remembering Christmases past.

Zechariah's Song in Luke, also called the Benedictus, turns us around to rehearse the past promises of God in anticipation and hope of God's imminent work in Jesus. God "spoke by the mouth of his holy prophets from of old, that we should be saved from our enemies... to show the mercy promised to our fathers and to remember his holy covenant, the oath that he swore to our father Abraham" (Luke 1:70-73). In Advent, we turn to face God's ultimate salvific act of remembrance in Jesus's incarnation, death, and resurrection.

Zechariah also points to a future hope. "And you, child, will be called the prophet of the Most High; for you will go before the Lord to prepare his ways, to give knowledge of salvation to his people in the forgiveness of their sins" (Luke 1:76-77). Likewise, as we face backward toward Christ's work for us, we look over our shoulders at what is to come. We have this knowledge of salvation by the forgiveness of sins now. But we await a time when sin and darkness are no more. We hope for what Christ has promised: his second Advent, or his return.

And our hope for the future is not without evidence: God's acts of mercy, love, and salvation on our behalf, which he showed most fully in the incarnation, life, death, and resurrection of Jesus, the Word made flesh (John 1:14) are delivered to us in word and sacrament. The season of Advent turns us around to walk backward into Christmas. We face the work of Christ's first coming as we anticipate his return.

Heavenly Father, we are poor, miserable sinners, undeserving of the riches of your kingdom. Yet, while we were still sinners, you promised to wash away all our sin. We give you thanks for the grace given to us through the work of your Son. Be with us as we look back at your promises fulfilled in Christ and given to us in baptism and communion. Amen.

FOR FURTHER REFLECTION, READ LUKE 1:68-79.

Glory in the Highest

AND AS HE RODE ALONG, THEY SPREAD THEIR CLOAKS ON THE ROAD. AS HE WAS DRAWING NEAR—ALREADY ON THE WAY DOWN THE MOUNT OF OLIVES—THE WHOLE MULTITUDE OF HIS DISCIPLES BEGAN TO REJOICE AND PRAISE GOD WITH A LOUD VOICE FOR ALL THE MIGHTY WORKS THAT THEY HAD SEEN, SAYING, "BLESSED IS THE KING WHO COMES IN THE NAME OF THE LORD! PEACE IN HEAVEN AND GLORY IN THE HIGHEST!"

—Luke 19:36-38

No, that is not a typo; you are still reading an Advent devotional. But why, on this, the first Monday of Advent, this first week of Advent, would we meditate on such texts? The triumphant entry of Jesus into the city of Jerusalem seems a better fit for the first Monday of Lent. In fact, this same text, which is historically designated for the first Sunday in Advent, appears again on Palm

Sunday, as the church begins her journey through Holy Week.

Jesus, having come to Jerusalem to celebrate the feast of the Passover, is greeted by a crowd singing the praises of he who comes in the name of the Lord. "Blessed is the King who comes in the name of the Lord! Peace in heaven and glory in the highest!" (Luke 19:38). The crowd outside Jerusalem glorifies Jesus's entry into the Holy City with a familiar song. We heard a song with a similar tone as the angels greeted the shepherds at Jesus's birth.

"And suddenly there was with the angel a multitude of the heavenly host praising God and saying, 'Glory to God in the highest, and on earth peace among those with whom he is pleased!'" (Luke 2:13-14).

The song of the angels parallels the crowd's greeting to Jesus as he humbly rode into Jerusalem to deliver the good news of the God who had made his arrival. And, the good news of Jesus's arrival is this: he will bring peace.

As we begin to prepare for Advent and Christmas, we set our eyes on Jesus who was born for us. We gaze upon the mystery of the incarnation this Advent, as we sing along with the song of the angels and of the crowd who came to greet him as he rode into Jerusalem. Glory to God in the highest!

At the start of this season, we not only contemplate the birth of Christ, we also behold his entry into Jerusalem. We behold his work for us, that we may have peace with God. We behold Jesus as he is born for us, crucified for us, and raised for us. Advent and Christmas are all about the work of Jesus for us.

Heavenly Father, as we prepare to celebrate the birth of your Son, help us meditate on the work he accomplished for us. Amen.

FOR FURTHER REFLECTION, READ LUKE 19:28-40.

Preparing the Way for Christmas

EVERY VALLEY SHALL BE LIFTED UP,
AND EVERY MOUNTAIN AND HILL MADE LOW;
THE UNEVEN GROUND SHALL BECOME LEVEL,
AND THE ROUGH PLACES A PLAIN.

—Isaiah 40:4

It feels like, as soon as our Thanksgiving meal is done and we wake up from our turkey-induced naps, a thousand different obstacles stand between us and Christmas.

Huge on the list for being ready for Christmas is putting up decorations. For many of us, we're not prepared until the tree is up and decorated and the lights on the house all work properly. This and other obstacles have to do with *us* preparing the way for Christmas. Through our efforts, we try to bring about Christmas as *we* think it should be.

Sometimes we fancy ourselves modern John the Baptists—voices crying out in the wilderness of Christmas consumerism, "Prepare ye the way of the Lord! Jesus is the reason for the season! It's Merry Christmas, not happy holidays!"

But does a yard sign reminding your neighbor (whom you don't talk to) that "Jesus is the reason for the season" lift up every valley and make low every mountain? Or does it make those valleys deeper and mountains higher? Does a snarky under-your-breath comment to the cashier wishing everyone (not just you) a happy holiday season make uneven ground level and rough places plain? Or does it make plain places rough and level places rocky?

Isaiah 40:3-4 is part of the gospel prophecy of John the Baptist and the message God called him to bring as the "voice" crying out to prepare the way for Jesus' coming. But often left out of our thinking is verse 5: "And the glory of the Lord shall be revealed and all flesh shall see it together, for the mouth of the Lord has spoken."

Who is it that prepares the way for Christmas? God himself, through his word. John did not make up his message; God gave it to him. God spoke his word through John.

Likewise, we do not prepare the way for Christmas. It comes whether we're ready or not. Rather, it is God who prepares us through his word. His word of law (his demands and commands) level us and our attempts at self-righteousness. His word of gospel (his promises fulfilled for us) fills in the valleys where we are empty.

God prepares us ultimately through his Word made flesh, Jesus, his Son, our forgiver, and our Lord. He prepares through the good news of his forgiving Word made flesh preached to us and given to us in the sacraments.

Heavenly Father, prepare us in this season of Advent to receive the good news of your Word, our Savior. Amen.

> **FOR FURTHER REFLECTION, READ ISAIAH 40:1-11.**

Waiting with the Light

WATCH THEREFORE, FOR YOU KNOW NEITHER THE DAY NOR THE HOUR.

—Matthew 25:13

Advent is a season of anticipation as we look for the second coming of Jesus, our incarnate and risen Lord.

Jesus expounded on watching and waiting for his return in parables. In the parable of the ten virgins, Jesus tells us of those who were waiting for the bridegroom to appear and make his grand entrance into the wedding feast. Five of those waiting brought oil to light their lamps for this monumental event. The other five were foolish and did not. The bridegroom was delayed so long that they all fell asleep. Then, the bridegroom appears.

With his audience in suspense as to what will happen next, Jesus continues with the parable. He tells them that the wise ones who had come prepared were welcomed into the grand wedding feast. However, sometime later the foolish ones came kicking on the door asking to enter (they had left in an attempt to find oil to purchase after the news of the bridegroom's imminent arrival). Jesus ends the parable with stunning words spoken to the foolish ones, "Truly, I say to you, I do not know you" (Matt. 25:12).

Our Lord is coming. He promised. But what of this parable? Should it frighten us? How do we prepare for our Lord's coming?

Jesus.

He's the answer. The foolish ones who do not have oil are foolish because they do not have the source of the light. The wise ones are wise only because they hold onto that light. They are both asleep when the bridegroom comes; however, what separates them is the light. "Again Jesus spoke to them, saying, 'I am the light of the world. Whoever follows me will not walk in darkness, but will have the light of life'" (John 8:12).

Through the waters of Holy Baptism, we have been given the light the world. Though we may fall asleep, not even the sleep of death can separate us from the light of Christ we have been given. The Lord cannot say to us that he does not know us because he, himself, has placed his holy name upon us.

Heavenly Father, as we wait and watch for the reappearing of your Son, may we be reminded of the promises you have made to us in the waters of Holy Baptism. Keep us in Christ, our light, that we may join with all the saints in the glorious wedding feast of the Lamb. Amen.

FOR FURTHER REFLECTION, READ MATTHEW 25:1-13.

God's Saving Patience

THE LORD IS NOT SLOW TO FULFILL HIS PROMISE AS SOME COUNT SLOWNESS, BUT IS PATIENT TOWARD YOU, NOT WISHING THAT ANY SHOULD PERISH, BUT THAT ALL SHOULD REACH REPENTANCE.

—2 Peter 3:9

God's kindness has a way of offending the self-righteous. We know the self-righteous as those who think they have done enough to be enough in God's eyes. But the self-righteous are also those who forget the kindness and grace God has shown to them and act as if they deserved it.

We see this second kind of self-righteousness in Jesus's parable of the unforgiving servant in Matthew 18:21-35. There, a servant is forgiven an insurmountable debt by his master. He, in turn, found a fellow servant who owed him a pittance in comparison to his now-forgiven debt and began to choke him and demand his money. When the fellow servant pleaded for patience, the forgiven servant refused and put him in prison.

The actions of the forgiven servant certainly offend our sensibilities. Rightly so. But we act like him. We may not lay hands on our neighbors, but we demand that they do right, if not by us, at least by God. We put them in the prison of our judgment for trying God's patience as if he needed us to defend it.

Paul writes in Romans 2:3-4, "Do you suppose, O man—you who judge those who practice such things and yet do them yourself—that you will escape the judgment of God? Or do you presume on the riches of his kindness and forbearance and patience, not knowing that God's kindness is meant to lead you to repentance?"

Of all the ways God's kindness could offend us, God's patience seems to offend us the most. Mostly because it seems as if God is doing nothing when he should be doing something. Namely, he should be doing something to stop someone else from doing wrong.

We forget that we were and are in need of God's long-suffering patience, his steadfast love and kindness. Without Jesus's work for us—his incarnation, death, and resurrection—we would perish. Without God's kindness on display in Christ, we would not be led to repentance, again and again.

God's patience offends our inner sinner because it means we do nothing for our salvation. It would rather we be working off the bad and working toward our own righteousness. But, thanks be to God, Christ has come. Because of him, we can "count the patience of the Lord as salvation" (2 Peter 3:15).

_____

Heavenly Father, we do not deserve the long-suffering patience you have shown to us in Christ. Forgive us for our self-righteousness and remember your promised mercy toward us. Daily renew us in your mercy and grant that we may forgive our neighbor as fully and freely as you have forgiven us in Christ. Amen.

FOR FURTHER REFLECTION, READ 2 PETER 3:8-15.

The Messenger and the Message

"THEREFORE MY PEOPLE SHALL KNOW MY NAME. THEREFORE IN THAT DAY THEY SHALL KNOW THAT IT IS I WHO SPEAK; HERE I AM."

—Isaiah 52:6

The prophet Isaiah wrote, "How beautiful upon the mountains are the feet of him who brings good news, who publishes peace, who brings good news of happiness, who publishes salvation, who says to Zion, 'Your God reigns'" (Isa. 52:7).

The messenger's feet are beautiful because of the word they bring: a word of good news, of hope, of joy, of peace, of love, of salvation, of God's reign. The word used for "good news" here in Isaiah is the Hebrew equivalent of the Greek word *euangelion*, often translated as "gospel" in the New Testament.

But what makes the gospel message so good is that it is more than just an announcement by a nameless messenger.

This messenger not only brings the word of God; this messenger *is* the Word of God. The Word, whom John says was with God in the beginning and by whom all things were made (John 1:1-3). The messenger is the Word who became flesh and lived among us (John 1:14). The messenger is Immanuel, God with us (Isa. 7:14).

God himself, the Word made flesh, comes to deliver the gospel message of comfort, peace, and salvation. Even more than that, the Word made flesh comes to do that which his words announce. In plain sight, the Son of God comes to comfort his people and redeem them. Before the eyes of all nations and before all the ends of the earth, he comes to bring us salvation.

During Advent and Christmas, we celebrate more than the historical event of Jesus's birth. We heed the words of Isaiah, "The voice of your watchmen—they lift up their voice; together they sing for joy; for eye to eye they see the return of the Lord to Zion. Break forth together into singing, you waste places of Jerusalem, for the Lord has comforted his people; he has redeemed Jerusalem. The Lord has bared his holy arm before the eyes of all the nations, and all the ends of the earth shall see the salvation of our God" (Isa. 52:8-10).

We lift our voices and sing for joy together as we celebrate the God who was, who is, and who will be with us.

The same God who came down into the burning bush, who promised, "I will be who I will be," that is, "I will be with you," and the same God who rescued Israel from slavery in Egypt, came down and took on human flesh in the incarnation. He not only came to be with us but came for us. Jesus, the enfleshed Word of God, came to redeem us from slavery to sin and bondage to death through his death and resurrection, and he will come again.

Heavenly Father, we give you thanks for those who bring the good news of your salvation to us. Make us messengers of the gospel as we proclaim the work your beloved Son has accomplished for us. Amen.

FOR FURTHER REFLECTION, READ ISAIAH 52:1-10.

The Fruit of Death

FOR AS THE EARTH BRINGS FORTH ITS SPROUTS, AND AS A GARDEN CAUSES WHAT IS SOWN IN IT TO SPROUT UP, SO THE LORD GOD WILL CAUSE RIGHTEOUSNESS AND PRAISE TO SPROUT UP BEFORE ALL THE NATIONS.

—*Isaiah 61:11*

Adam and Eve, the man and woman God made, stared at each other. They knew something was wrong. They gathered up leaves to make clothing for themselves. Then, they hid among more leaves as they heard God approach.

They did the one thing God told them not to do. In doing so, they brought death into the world. And what exactly their next moments held, they did not know. Their future became a terrifying mystery.

But then came hope in a promise from their creator.

God promised a seed, an offspring of Eve, the mother of all living (Gen. 3:20), to crush death and death's forebear, the devil, and bring forth life and righteousness to all people.

But how does one crush death *and* bring forth life?

Out of the earthen man and woman who brought death into the world, God would bring life. Out of Mary, who, as a virgin, could not bring forth life, God would bring forth the seed promised to Adam and Eve.

Jesus said, "Truly, truly, I say to you, unless a grain of wheat falls into the earth and dies, it remains alone; but if it dies it bears much fruit" (John 12:24). Through his own death, Jesus, the promised seed, would crush death.

Out of the death of that promised seed on the cross and his earthen burial, God would cause fruit to grow. As God caused new life in Mary, so too does he bring forth new life and righteousness for you through the resurrection of his Son.

And so we sing, "Hail the heav'n-born Prince of Peace! Hail the sun of righteousness! Light and life to all he brings, Ris'n with healing in his wings. Mild he lays his glory by, Born that we no more may die, Born to raise each child of earth, Born to give us second birth."[1]

---

[1] Wesley, Charles. *Lutheran Book of Worship*. Minneapolis, MN: Augsburg Pub. House, 1978, 60.

Heavenly Father, in the weaknesses of this world, in those weaknesses found in us, show us your strength. Remind us you can bring life out of death and that out of Jesus's death you bring life to all. Amen.

FOR FURTHER REFLECTION, READ ISAIAH 61:1-4, 8-11.

The SECOND WEEK *of* ADVENT

The God Who Regards Me

FOR HE HAS LOOKED ON THE HUMBLE ESTATE OF HIS SERVANT. FOR BEHOLD, FROM NOW ON ALL GENERATIONS WILL CALL ME BLESSED; FOR HE WHO IS MIGHTY HAS DONE GREAT THINGS FOR ME, AND HOLY IS HIS NAME.

—Luke 1:48-49

There was nothing special about her. She was a less-than-ordinary girl from a small backwater town. There was no reason to assume anything significant would become of her in her lifetime. The world power of the day, Rome, had overtaken her people and she was bound to reside at the bottom of the social ladder, as a woman and as a Jew.

As far as her relationship with God was concerned, she was also seemingly last in line. Although her ancestor was the great King David, she now was just part of a poor family trying to put food on the table. She had nothing—no title, power, money, fame, or social status. Nothing about her in the eyes of the world would merit a second glance from the God of Abraham, Isaac, and Jacob.

This girl, Mary, was much like another woman we read about in the Old Testament. Her name was Hannah. She too was a poor Israelite who had nothing of substance to offer to God; yet, God regarded her. God gave her who was barren a son and she rejoiced in the God who heard her cries and looked with favor on her (1 Sam. 2:1-10).

God looked with favor on these two women, and they both burst into song. Their songs are strikingly similar though they are generations apart. They sing of the God who has seen them, who has regarded them despite their low estate. The only significant thing they had to offer God was their sin.

Luther remarks about Mary's song, "Mary confesses that the foremost work God did for her was that he regarded her, which is indeed the greatest of his works, on which all the rest depend and from which they all derive."[2] God regarded two sinners and looked on them with favor. He looked on them with Jesus.

We can join the songs of Mary and Hannah this Advent. We can confess along with them the God who has regarded us. We can sing of the God who looks with favor on us, who turns his face towards us in the Word made flesh. God has regarded us

---

[2] Luther, Martin, and Pelikan, Jaroslav. *Luther's Works: Sermon on the Mount and the Magnificat*. Vol. 21. Saint Louis: Concordia, 1956, 321.

in our baptism as he places his name on us. In the sacrament of the altar, our Lord does not deny or betray us but welcomes us as his guests and forgives us all our sins as we are given his very body and blood.

Heavenly Father, you have not turned your face from us in our sin and unbelief but have turned toward us in love through the work of your Son. Look with favor on us this Advent season and remind us of the promises you have made and will keep in Christ for our benefit. Amen.

> **FOR FURTHER REFLECTION, READ LUKE 1:46-55.**

Swaddling Cloths

AND SHE GAVE BIRTH TO HER FIRSTBORN SON
AND WRAPPED HIM IN SWADDLING CLOTHS AND
LAID HIM IN A MANGER, BECAUSE THERE WAS
NO PLACE FOR THEM IN THE INN.

—Luke 2:7

When Luke sits down to write his Gospel account, he does not start by examining the genealogy of Jesus as Matthew had, but rather spills more ink as he brings to life the account of Jesus's birth.

Luke is determined to collect all the details from eyewitnesses to Jesus and authenticate their credibility. He sets out on this endeavor so that we, as Luke himself said, "may have certainty concerning the things you have been taught" (Luke 1:4).

We are not told the specifics of who these eyewitnesses are, but we are given hints as to who may have sat down with

Luke to retell the glorious birth, ministry, death, and resurrection of Christ. Luke goes into more specifics about the birth of Jesus and even states that "Mary treasured up all these things, pondering them in her heart" (Luke 2:19).

In the second chapter of Luke's account, he writes that Mary "gave birth to her firstborn son and wrapped him in swaddling cloths and laid him in a manger, because there was no place for them in the inn" (Luke 2:7). As Luke penned the Christmas story, he also had at the ready the accounts of Jesus's death and resurrection.

Near the end of his account, Luke paints with his narrative a similar likeness of the Christ swaddled in cloths and laid to rest. As we page ahead in Luke's account, there is an absence of a joyful song. Instead of a sky bright with multitudes of angels, the sky is dark as Jesus dies (Luke 23:44). And, just as Jesus was wrapped in swaddling cloths, Luke records for us that he was wrapped in linen and laid in a tomb (Luke 23:52-53).

Before the ink has set on the page, Luke immediately continues to tell us of the disciples who had gone to the tomb wherein Jesus was laid. They found it empty with the exception of the linen that had swaddled our crucified Lord, now risen (Luke 24:12).

We soon will celebrate the birth of our Lord and see the baby Jesus swaddled in cloths and lying in the manger of our nativity sets. But Jesus is no longer swaddled in cloths nor wrapped in strips of linen. Jesus can no longer be found in the manger of Bethlehem, any more than he can be found in the tomb.

Jesus instead has wrapped himself up in the waters of baptism and laid himself in our mouths in the bread and wine of his holy supper. Merry Christmas, he is risen, he is risen indeed!

Heavenly Father, we give you thanks for your Word to joyfully hear and learn. May we joyfully receive your Son and the comfort of the forgiveness of our sins as we celebrate his birth. Amen.

FOR FURTHER REFLECTION, READ LUKE 24:1-12.

He Will Do It

NOW MAY THE GOD OF PEACE HIMSELF
SANCTIFY YOU COMPLETELY, AND MAY YOUR
WHOLE SPIRIT AND SOUL AND BODY BE KEPT
BLAMELESS AT THE COMING OF OUR LORD
JESUS CHRIST. HE WHO CALLS YOU IS FAITHFUL;
HE WILL SURELY DO IT.

—1 Thessalonians 5:23-24

In 1 Thessalonians 5:16-22, Paul gives a list of things to do—a pretty agreeable list at that.

"Rejoice always, pray without ceasing, give thanks in all circumstances; for this is the will of God in Christ Jesus for you. Do not quench the Spirit. Do not despise prophecies, but test everything; hold fast what is good. Abstain from every form of evil."

Don't do evil? Raise your hand if you think that's a good idea. Hold fast to what is good? In this day and age, how does anyone get through the day without doing that? Test everything? That's a good idea. We *should* know if someone is telling the truth or trying to pull the wool over our eyes.

Don't quench the Spirit? We might not know what that means on first reading, but it sounds like something we should avoid doing, right? God's will for us is to be thankful in all circumstances? Who wouldn't want to be content no matter what life throws at them?

You may be asking, "What's wrong with the list? You wouldn't have brought up the list unless there was a problem." Nothing is wrong with the list. The problem is with us.

We sinners have a habit of turning these imperatives, these things to do, these commands of God into something we need to do to earn God's love and grace. If not to earn it, then at least to show that we are worthy enough to remain loved by God.

We think things like, "God has saved me. But I need to show my gratitude. I need to always rejoice, always listen to his word and talk with him, and always do his will. God has made me holy, but I need to stay holy. Or else..."

Paul says otherwise. He preaches good news to us, lest these laws burden us. It is God who sanctifies us completely, that is, he makes us holy. It is he who keeps us—body, soul, and spirit—blameless (read holy) until Jesus appears again. He tells us, "He who calls you is faithful; he will surely do it." As God faithfully sent his Son as he promised, so too will he keep us until he sends him again.

Heavenly Father, remind us always of your faithfulness to us when we are faithless. By your Holy Spirit, guard and keep us in the faith that we may be kept blameless at the coming of our Lord Jesus Christ. Amen.

> **FOR FURTHER REFLECTION,**
> **READ 1 THESSALONIANS 5:16-24.**

Holding onto the Promise

LORD, NOW YOU ARE LETTING YOUR SERVANT
DEPART IN PEACE, ACCORDING TO YOUR WORD;
FOR MY EYES HAVE SEEN YOUR SALVATION.

—Luke 2:29-30

We're not sure how long he had been waiting. He was not told how long he must wait; he was only given a promise. He was promised that, as the evangelist Luke writes, "he would not see death before he had seen the Lord's Christ" (Luke 2:26).

He did not know the day or time, but he was confident he would see the Christ, the consolation of Israel, with his own eyes. It must happen. Because God said so.

Simeon was going to meet his Savior face to face; it was a guarantee made solely by his God. And the promises of God are unshakeable. There was nothing in Simeon that prompted this promise to be given to him. Likewise, there were no criteria or prerequisites Simeon had to meet in order for the fulfillment of the word to occur.

Martin Luther writes this regarding the promises of our God, "When God makes a promise, there he himself is dealing with us and is giving and offering us something...The promise is certain and reliable, and is surely carried out, because God carries it out."[3]

Simeon held onto the promise until, on the eighth day of Jesus's life, he held that promise in his arms. When Jesus is brought to the temple by Mary and Joseph, Simeon holds the promised Messiah, the one who had been promised to Adam and Eve, to Abraham, Isaac, and Jacob, and to himself. As priests were in the temple that day, he holds the infant Christ, the greater priest. Jesus, our great high priest, had come.

Simeon cannot contain his joy and bursts into song. It is like a wondrous, unrestrained "amen" to the promise he had been waiting to see. It is the response "this is most certainly true" to the revelation of the Holy Spirit. Simeon's song is the fruit of faith worked out by the Holy Spirit as he holds the promise.

We behold the comfort and consolation of sinners every time the Lord gives us his gifts in Word and sacrament. We cannot hold the infant Christ in our arms, but his body and blood for

---

[3] Luther, Martin, and Pelikan, Jaroslav. *Luther's Works: Lectures on Genesis Chapters 15-20.* Vol.3. Saint Louis: Concordia, 1961, 24, 26.

the forgiveness of our sins are cradled in our mouths as he gives to us the promise of everlasting life. The prophet Isaiah writes, "The grass withers, the flower fades, but the word of our God will stand forever" (Isa. 40:8). God keeps his promises.

Heavenly Father, you keep your promises. By the work of the Holy Spirit, keep us in the true faith, in the work of your Son. Comfort us with your promises of forgiveness and everlasting life, through Christ our Lord. Amen.

FOR FURTHER REFLECTION, READ LUKE 2:25-32.

Our Righteousness, Our Enoughness

IN THOSE DAYS JUDAH WILL BE SAVED,
AND JERUSALEM WILL DWELL SECURELY.
AND THIS IS THE NAME BY WHICH IT WILL
BE CALLED: "THE LORD IS OUR
RIGHTEOUSNESS."

—Jeremiah 33:16

The term "righteousness" can feel stuffy and outdated to the modern ear. We certainly know we don't want to be self-righteous. But, still, its definition feels elusive. We know it when we see it, but can't quite put it into words.

A simple definition of being righteous or having righteousness is being in or having a right relationship with God. But David Zahl, in his book *Seculosity*, provides an accessible synonym that more easily translates into our everyday lives: enoughness.[4]

This "enoughness" plays out in anything and everything we use to justify our thoughts, words, and actions in the face of judgment and criticism. We use it to measure our worthiness in the eyes of others and ourselves. We try to prove that we work hard enough, parent well enough, eat well enough, vacation well enough, vote well enough, love well enough, and on and on. We try to show we are worthy parents, spouses, and coworkers. That we are worthy human beings.

The problem that Zahl outlines is that we have moved where we find our enoughness, our righteousness, as it were, from the vertical (in God) to the horizontal (in the things of this world). We search for security, salvation, and assurance among the things around us.

But this problem is nothing new. It plagued Jeremiah's original hearers too. When things got tough, they forsook faith in God to trust in things around them—their wealth, their kings, and foreign powers, to name a few. Yet, God did not forsake his promise to his people. They would be saved and dwell securely, and they would be named, "The Lord is our righteousness."

God accomplished this through the one of whom Jeremiah would say, "Behold, the days are coming declares the Lord,

---

[4] Zahl, David. *Seculosity: How Career, Parenting, Technology, Food, Politics, and Romance Became Our New Religion and What to Do about It.* Fortress Press, 2019. xvi.

when I will raise up for David a righteous Branch and he shall reign as king and deal wisely, and shall execute justice and righteousness in the land. In his days, Judah will be saved, and Israel will dwell securely. And this is the name by which he will be called: 'The Lord is our righteousness'" (Jer. 23:5-6).

This promise is for you too. It is guaranteed through Jesus, who is your righteousness from God (1 Cor. 1:30). He came to be enough for you and to give you that which you could never be yourself: enough in the eyes of your Heavenly Father. In and through Christ, you are worthy.

Heavenly Father, you sent your only Son into this world to take away our unrighteousness, our sin. We thank you that, through baptism, you have clothed us in the righteousness and work of your Son, and given us peace and eternal life with you. Amen.

FOR FURTHER REFLECTION, READ JEREMIAH 33:14-16.

How the Promised Shepherd Shepherds

AND HE SHALL STAND AND SHEPHERD HIS FLOCK IN THE STRENGTH OF THE LORD, IN THE MAJESTY OF THE NAME OF THE LORD HIS GOD. AND THEY SHALL DWELL SECURE, FOR NOW HE SHALL BE GREAT TO THE ENDS OF THE EARTH. AND HE SHALL BE THEIR PEACE.

—Micah 5:4-5a

After Jesus was born, some wise men or magi came to Herod, the king of Israel at that time, and asked, "Where is he who has been born king of the Jews?" (Matt. 2:2). Herod, in a paranoid panic, summoned the chief priests and scribes to quickly find out.

They answered, "In Bethlehem of Judea, for so it is written by the prophet: 'And you, O Bethlehem, in the land of Judah, are by no means least among the rulers of Judah; for from you shall come a ruler who will shepherd my people Israel.'"

These words are part of a prophecy spoken by the prophet Micah. Matthew connects this promise to Jesus, the promised son of David, the David who was both a shepherd and a king. Micah goes on to say that the shepherd will be his flock's peace and that they shall dwell secure for he will, "shepherd his flock in the strength of the Lord" (Mic. 5:4-5a).

What does it mean to shepherd in the strength of the Lord? Does it look like a great show of strength? A terrifying display of power? A back-breaking, will-breaking act of aggression?

We might think that. After all, that's how we rule and lead each other. Governments intimidate each other with shows of strength. They enforce laws often with postures and power moves. They signal their ability to kill and destroy. Perhaps this is how this Shepherd-King will rule.

But that is not how this shepherd will shepherd. Nor how this king will rule.

In John 10:10-11, Jesus, the promised shepherd-king, says, "The thief comes only to steal and kill and destroy. I came that they may have life and have it abundantly. I am the good shepherd. The good shepherd lays down his life for the sheep."

This is how the Christ—born in Bethlehem, the city of the first great shepherd-king of Israel, David—shepherds and leads us. He came to give us abundant life, eternal life, by laying down *his* life for us.

On the cross, we see how the promised shepherd shepherds. He does not crush us or seek to destroy us. He was crushed for us, for our sins (Isa. 53:5). He leads the way to life through his death. In him, we dwell secure because, by his death, we are forgiven. By his death, he is our peace.

Heavenly Father, draw our eyes to Christ on the cross to see how you shepherd us. Not in wrath and vengeance, but in grace and mercy through the death and resurrection of your incarnate Word. Amen.

FOR FURTHER REFLECTION, READ MICAH 5:2-5A.

Location, Location, Location

HE WILL BE GREAT AND WILL BE CALLED
THE SON OF THE MOST HIGH. AND THE
LORD GOD WILL GIVE TO HIM THE THRONE
OF HIS FATHER DAVID.

—Luke 1:32

From the beginning and throughout the Old Testament, God constantly concerns himself with the location of his creatures.

God's ultimate concern for the location of his people comes down to how closely they reside to him. Before the first sin, Adam and Eve walked with God unhindered in the garden. As the Israelites wandered in the wilderness, God placed himself among his rescued people in the tabernacle. But their unholiness limited their access to him. As with the tabernacle, so it went with the temple in Jerusalem. God's holiness held the unholy back.

In one sentence from the angel Gabriel, we see how God intends to change that dilemma. The son Mary will have, conceived through the power of the Holy Spirit, will be the Son of the Most High, that is the God of Adam, Eve, and Abraham, the God who rescued his people out of slavery in Egypt. He will also sit on the throne of his father David.

When David was finally at peace as the king of Israel and God had given him rest, he decided God needed a better home, a nicer location to dwell in. David had a nice home. God should have a nice house too. But God had a different plan.

He told David through the prophet Nathan, "The Lord declares to you that the Lord will make you a house.... I will raise up your offspring after you, who shall come from your body, and I will establish his kingdom. He shall build a house for my name, and I will establish the throne of his kingdom forever" (2 Sam. 7:11-13).

The promised Savior and King will have two lineages: one divine, the other human. He will be God and man united together. Inseparable. In the son of David, God and humanity will dwell together forever.

Jesus's incarnation restored God's proper place among his creatures. God relocated to dwell with us. He also relocates us. Jesus's death and resurrection take us from our self-built shanties of sin and put us in the Father's hallowed halls as his children, and as saints forever.

As the writer of the book of Hebrews reminds us, "Therefore, brothers, since we have confidence to enter the holy places by the blood of Jesus... let us draw near with a true heart in full assurance of faith, with our hearts sprinkled clean from an evil conscience and our bodies washed with pure water" (Heb. 10:19, 22).

Heavenly Father, by the death and resurrection of Jesus, the Son of the Most High and the promised son of David, you bring us to dwell with you. May we enter your presence this Advent and Christmas season with thanksgiving and praise. Amen.

FOR FURTHER REFLECTION, READ 2 SAMUEL 7:1-11, 16.

The THIRD WEEK *of* ADVENT

For Unto You This Day

GLORY TO GOD IN THE HIGHEST,
AND ON EARTH PEACE AMONG THOSE
WITH WHOM HE IS PLEASED!

—Luke 2:14

Many of us go through life having little reason to believe God is pleased with us. Despite our baptism and despite how hard we try, we can't quite seem to quit sinning. We never manage to move past our ability to mess up.

The shepherds had just as many reasons to think that God was displeased with them as we do. Though the great King David was a shepherd, by the time of Jesus's birth, they were not the elite. They were not respectably employed since they worked at night. They were the maligned and marginalized of society. Counted as less.

If you were a shepherd, you were probably one because you couldn't do much else. Either you lacked the skills to do another job, or your sins against society forced you to hide out on the night shift, away from most people.

That the angels came to shepherds first was not a matter of convenience, but a matter of intention. "For unto you this day is born a Savior." Unto whom? Not unto those who have it all figured out, the self-righteous on whom society's favor rests, but unto the sinner on whom God's favor rests on account of the Savior born in Bethlehem.

This Savior would grow up to be the Good Shepherd who would say that he had not come for the righteous but for the shepherd and the tax collector, the prostitute and the poor. He came for sinners (Mark 2:17). He came for you.

By his birth, life, death, and resurrection he brings peace on earth to us who make discord. He unites heaven with earth, God with humanity, sinners with their Savior. No matter how frequent our sins, no matter how often we repeat them, no matter how many intentions to be better we break, we are forgiven.

God is pleased with us on account of Christ, the Son with whom he is well pleased. He is pleased with you today—not for anything you did, but because a Savior was born for you.

Heavenly Father, you are pleased with us not on account of our actions, but on account of the perfect life, death, and resurrection of your Son in our place. Keep us in this faith and forgiveness of sins you have freely given to us in our baptism. Amen.

FOR FURTHER REFLECTION, READ LUKE 2:8-20.

The Silent Word

WHO IS TO CONDEMN? CHRIST JESUS IS THE
ONE WHO DIED—MORE THAN THAT, WHO WAS
RAISED—WHO IS AT THE RIGHT HAND OF GOD,
WHO INDEED IS INTERCEDING FOR US.

—Romans 8:34

The little village of Bethlehem was bustling with out-of-town guests. It was anything but a silent night as weary travelers packed their families into any and every available guest room in town. It was a reunion for anyone and everyone who had come from King David's family, although this wasn't your typical family reunion. This was a reunion called for by Caesar himself, and not for sentimental reasons. Caesar set a decree that the entire Roman world must register for a census.

The timing of such an event couldn't have been more inconvenient. With the journey to Bethlehem complete for the engaged couple and shelter for their stay figured out, it was suddenly time. The Gospel writer Luke tells us that during their stay in Bethlehem, the time came for Mary to give birth (Luke 2:6).

The overcrowded yet lowly town of Bethlehem beheld the sacred baby cradled in a manger. While the Roman government calculated and curated a report for Caesar, the Word made flesh laid nestled in the arms of his mother.

The hymn writer William C. Dix ponders this divine occasion in his hymn, *What Child Is This*. In the second verse of his hymn, Dix proclaims the priestly work of this baby born to Mary. Dix writes, "for sinners here the silent Word is pleading."[5]

The prophet Isaiah writes, "All we like sheep have gone astray; we have turned—every one—to his own way; and the Lord has laid on him the iniquity of us all. He was oppressed, and he was afflicted, yet he opened not his mouth; like a lamb that is led to the slaughter, and like a sheep that before its shearers is silent, so he opened not his mouth" (Isa. 53:6-7).

Jesus has come to plead for us in his perfect life and sacrificial death for us that we may be rescued from sin and death. From the quiet slumber of the Christ child to the silence he kept as he was charged and died for our sins, the sinless Son of God pleads for us.

Through the silence of Christ, God silenced our enemies. No more can Satan accuse you of your sin, for your sin is buried with Christ and you have been raised with him in the waters of Holy Baptism.

---

[5] Dix, William C. *Lutheran Service Book: Pew Edition.* Saint Louis, MO: Concordia Publishing House, 2006, 370.

Heavenly Father, to our sin and suffering you did not remain silent. You sent your Son that he may make atonement for our sins and sit at your right hand as our intercessor. May our Advent meditations point us ever to Christ and his work for us. Amen.

FOR FURTHER REFLECTION, READ ISAIAH 53:1-12.

The Coming of the King

WHERE IS HE WHO HAS BEEN BORN KING OF THE JEWS? FOR WE SAW HIS STAR WHEN IT ROSE AND HAVE COME TO WORSHIP HIM.

—Matthew 2:2

The hymns and readings in Advent swell with language and imagery of a coming king and his kingdom. In his Gospel account, Matthew tells of magi from the east who came to worship the newborn king of the Jews. The voice of John the Baptizer leaps from the page as he proclaims, "Repent, for the kingdom of heaven is at hand" (Matt. 3:2).

Jesus speaks of himself in a kingly manner. When he speaks in parables, he conveys a great deal about the kingdom of God. The first week of Advent, we hear of Jesus riding into Jerusalem, greeted with a jubilant song, "Blessed is the King who comes in the name of the Lord!" (Luke 19:38). The King's coronation day was coming.

While a glorious King to us, his people, he is a laughable king to the world. Instead of a crown of gold, he is crowned with thorns. Rather than the praise and adoration of the crowds, he is spat upon and blasphemed. Rather than holding a lustrous gold scepter in hand, nails hold his hands to the cross.

The kingship of Christ is alien to the decorum of the kings of this world. Norman Nagel describes the kingship of Christ in this way: "The kingship of Christ was not in Galilean shouts for the hometown man who had become a public figure. It was in our Lord's eyes when He turned to Peter. It was in our Lord's voice when He said 'Mary' to the weeping Magdalene."[6]

Our King's work is deeply personal. Christ, our King, is not far off. Our Lord comes to become our sin, to die, for us. The kingship of Christ is immersed with the comfort of sins forgiven, and bound up in the cross—for you!

The hallmark of our King is not in the praise of the crowds, but in his work for our salvation on Calvary. He comes and rules with mercy and grace. The king born in Bethlehem is born that he may redeem and comfort you and bring you to everlasting life.

---

[6] Nagel, N. *Selected Sermons of Norman Nagel.* St Louis, MO: Concordia Publishing House, 2004, 120.

Heavenly Father, bring us at last with all the saints around the throne of the Lamb that we may sing the praise of our King forever and ever. Amen.

FOR FURTHER REFLECTION, READ MICAH 5:1-15.

According to His Word

AND MARY SAID, "BEHOLD, I AM THE SERVANT OF THE LORD; LET IT BE TO ME ACCORDING TO YOUR WORD."

—Luke 1:38

Our response to life-changing news depends on the circumstances. Mary was told that she would bear a child and he would be the Son of the Most High, the fulfillment of the promise made to David that a king would come from his family and reign forever.

This is good news. But the child would not be that of her betrothed, Joseph. Though a virgin, she would conceive through the power of the Holy Spirit. And she would be pregnant before she was officially married.

This was not such good news. In fact, it could reasonably be considered bad news. It meant she would likely be ostracized from her community, maybe even her family. In the eyes of her neighbors, she would bring shame on herself, her future husband, her family, and anyone else who chose to associate with her.

Mary's words have inspired numerous generations of Christians. But it is not a pie-in-the-sky, silver-lining-seeking, look-on-the-bright-side response. She doesn't muster her words out of blind enthusiasm or ignorant optimism.

During Advent, much of the world around us demands spirits of cheer and happy smiles. Perhaps during no other time of the year is there a collective sense demanding "joyful" perfection. The perfect gifts given and received with the right amount of gratitude. Perfect meals, perfectly enjoyed by family members getting along perfectly. The perfect feeling felt at the candlelight service, with the perfect amount of humility and sober joy.

But Advent comes to us in the midst of the dark days of winter. It comes to us in the nitty-gritty realities of life, scarred and marred by sin and its effects. That broken relationship that won't ever seem to be fixed. The empty seat at the table, whether for the first year or the fifteenth.

Mary responds through faith. But her faith is not optimistic or wishful thinking. It is a gift that God has given to her. It is in response to the God who is with her in the face of the encroaching shadows of dark times that she says, "Let it be to me according to your word."

We can respond in kind, even when we don't feel the joy that accompanies this season. Though we live in this vale of tears, nevertheless, because of Jesus's death and resurrection, we can say, "Let it be to me according to your word, your Word made flesh, your Word made flesh that died for my sins, your Word that declares me forgiven."

Heavenly Father, may it be to me according to your Word incarnate, crucified, and risen for me, whether I stand in the face of bright days or the shadow of dark ones. Amen.

FOR FURTHER REFLECTION, READ LUKE 1:26-38.

The Gospel of God's Name

BUT MOSES SAID TO GOD, "WHO AM I THAT
I SHOULD GO TO PHARAOH AND BRING THE
CHILDREN OF ISRAEL OUT OF EGYPT?" HE SAID,
"BUT I WILL BE WITH YOU."

—Exodus 3:11-12a

Our names carry weight. We sign our names to legal documents that make binding agreements. We're embarrassed when we forget the name of someone we see every week. Parents often talk to their children about living up to the family name. God's name is no different. It, too, carries power. The power of a promise only God can make.

In Exodus 3, God physically appears to Moses, in a burning bush. God tells Moses he is going to use him to set the Israelites free from slavery in Egypt. But Moses answers, "Who am I that I should go to Pharaoh and bring the children of Israel out of Egypt?" God answers Moses, "I will be with you" (Ex. 3:12).

Moses, always ready with an excuse, counters with another question. "If I come to the people of Israel and say to them, 'The God of your fathers has sent me to you,' and they ask me, 'What is his name?' what shall I say to them?" God answers Moses, "I will be who I will be." Or, more commonly translated, "I AM WHO I AM" (Ex. 3:14).

The word translated "I will be" is used in both places. First, in God's assurance to Moses that he *will be* with him and then again when God is telling Moses he will be who he will be.

The context in which God gives his name tells us that he has no intention of being a god who simply exists somewhere far off. He isn't just milling about, twiddling his thumbs, waiting for us to call on him or for things to get bad enough to intervene. He is not the God who turns away from us. He is the God who is with his people.

This is the gospel of God's name: that he is the God who draws near to you despite our failures to live up to his family name. This he does by putting his name on us in the waters of baptism. His name is a word of promise. "I AM who I AM and I will be who I will be, that is, I will be with you because I am for you. And I've sent my Son to show you."

Thanks be to God! When our names fail, God's name never does.

Heavenly Father, we give you thanks that you are not a god who is far off, but the God who is near to us and who does everything for our eternal good. Remind us daily of your promises to us fulfilled in your only begotten Son. Amen.

FOR FURTHER REFLECTION, READ EXODUS 3:1-14.

The Purifier

BEHOLD, I SEND MY MESSENGER, AND HE WILL
PREPARE THE WAY BEFORE ME. AND THE LORD
WHOM YOU SEEK WILL SUDDENLY COME TO
HIS TEMPLE; AND THE MESSENGER OF THE
COVENANT IN WHOM YOU DELIGHT, BEHOLD, HE
IS COMING, SAYS THE LORD OF HOSTS...HE WILL
SIT AS A REFINER AND PURIFIER OF SILVER,
AND HE WILL PURIFY THE SONS OF LEVI AND
REFINE THEM LIKE GOLD AND SILVER

—Malachi 3:1, 3

Throughout the Old Testament, specifically the book of
Leviticus, we learn of the etiquette of cleanliness. The life
of Israel was divided into what was clean and what was
unclean. Nothing unclean dared enter the premise of the
temple of the Lord, for the Lord is holy. The priests, the
sons of Levi, also called Levites, were not exempt from the
laws of cleanliness. They upheld the strictest purification
laws as priests to the Lord.

The prophet Malachi had some harsh words from the Lord for the Levites, "But you have turned aside from the way. You have caused many to stumble by your instruction. You have corrupted the covenant of Levi, says the Lord of hosts" (Mal. 2:8). The priests, with all of their purification ordinances, were themselves corrupt and unclean.

Additionally, they had to continually offer sacrifices for a perpetually sinful people. The rhythm of the temple followed the pattern of making what was unclean, clean—year after year, generation after generation.

After delivering the Lord's rebukes, Malachi brings the announcement that the Lord, himself, will come to his temple. The one who would disrupt the rhythm of purification in the Levitical priesthood, who would once and for all purify the sons of Levi.

The writer of the book of Hebrews echoes the words of the prophet Malachi, writing of their fulfillment. "After making purification for sins, he sat down at the right hand of the Majesty on high" (Heb. 1:3). The one who would sit as the refiner has come. The one who would purify the sons of Levi that they may bring offerings in righteousness to the Lord has appeared.

In the small town of Bethlehem, the Lord suddenly came to his temple. He, himself, was the temple, and our great High Priest. He offered himself as the sacrifice for our sin in the fire of

God's judgment so we may be purified of our unrighteousness through himself.

Jesus has finished the work of the refiner; we are made pure and holy, just as the Lord of hosts said. In Holy Baptism, with the water and the word, he has purified us from all our sin and unrighteousness. As we celebrate the coming of Christ, we celebrate and welcome our good and gracious High Priest who does all things for us.

Heavenly Father, we confess that we are poor miserable sinners. But you have not left us; in your mercy, you sent your Son for us. We thank you for the priestly work of your Son for our purification and salvation. Amen.

FOR FURTHER REFLECTION, READ 1 PETER 2:1-12.

The Face of God

RESTORE US, O LORD GOD OF HOSTS! LET YOUR
FACE SHINE, THAT WE MAY BE SAVED!

—Psalm 80:19

Three times, the psalmist makes this plea in Psalm 80.
"Restore us... Let your face shine, that we may be saved!"
In between those pleas, the psalmist recounts Israel's
dark situation. It is attacked, its defenses are down, and
it is the object of their neighbor's scorn, ridicule, and
contempt.

Worse still, God seems angry with Israel's prayers. They
eat and drink nothing but tears. "You have fed them with
the bread of tears and given them tears to drink in full
measure" (Ps. 80:5). Yet, the psalmist turns again to the
Lord. "Restore us, O Lord God of hosts!" This could also
read, "turn us again" or "repent us."

Eventually, the psalmist prays, "But let your hand be on
the man of your right hand, the son of man whom you
have made strong for yourself! Then we shall not turn

back from you; give us life, and we will call upon your name!" (Ps. 80:17-18).

Here, we see shades of Jesus. But there is more. Jesus is the face of God who shines on us. As he said to one of his disciples, "Whoever has seen me has seen the Father" (John 14:9). And as John, the apostle, writes, "In him was life, and the life was the light of men. The light shines in the darkness, and the darkness has not overcome it.... The true light, which gives light to everyone, was coming into the world" (John 1:4-5, 9).

This shining light is what God prophesied through the sorcerer-for-hire Balaam. "I behold him, but not near: a star shall come out of Jacob" (Num. 24:17). And Zechariah announced its imminent arrival at the birth of his son, John the Baptist. "The sunrise shall visit us from on high to give light to those who sit in darkness and in the shadow of death (Luke 1:78-79).

Furthermore, the words of the psalmist echo that of the blessing God gave to be spoken over his people, "The Lord bless you and keep you; the Lord make his face to shine upon you and be gracious to you; the Lord lift up his face and give you peace" (Num. 6:24-26).

In Jesus, the face of God, we see this promise come true. The light, which gives light and life to all, came into the world under attack by its enemies: sin, death, and the devil. In Jesus, God looks upon us with favor. Through Christ, we are repented; he turns us back to him. The shining face of God restores us, saves us, and gives us peace.

Heavenly Father, bless us and keep us in Christ; make your face shine on us through him; be gracious to us, look upon us with favor and give us peace because of his work for us. Amen.

FOR FURTHER REFLECTION, READ PSALM 80:1-19.

The FOURTH WEEK *of* ADVENT

He Who Comes to Us Comes for Us

AND THOSE WHO WENT BEFORE AND THOSE WHO FOLLOWED WERE SHOUTING, "HOSANNA! BLESSED IS HE WHO COMES IN THE NAME OF THE LORD! BLESSED IS THE COMING KINGDOM OF OUR FATHER DAVID! HOSANNA IN THE HIGHEST!"

—Mark 11:9-10

Jesus's triumphal entry into Jerusalem on the first day of the week of his death seems out of place in Advent, a season that prepares us to celebrate his birth. But because Advent rehearses Christ's first coming in anticipation of his second, this "Lent" event of the past gives us hope during Advent today.

People surrounded Jesus as he entered Jerusalem. Voices went before him and followed him, shouting, "Hosanna!"

They cry out for the salvation God promised he would send with the one who brings the everlasting kingdom of their forefather David—the salvation riding into Jerusalem before their eyes. But those who went before Jesus that day, raising their voices, were not the first to proclaim this message, nor were those who followed the last to sing this praise.

Before the Son of God became incarnate and rode into Jerusalem, the Old Testament people of God and the prophets declared that he would come. They clung to Moses's words, "The Lord your God will raise up for you a prophet like me from among you, from your brothers—it is to him you shall listen" (Deut. 18:15). They cried out with the psalmist, "Save us, we pray, O Lord! O Lord, we pray, give us success! Blessed is he who comes in the name of the Lord! We bless you from the house of the Lord" (Ps. 118:25-26).

Following the death, resurrection, and ascension of Jesus, the Apostles and the early church proclaimed the good news: the kingdom had come in Jesus. "But what God foretold by the mouth of all the prophets, that his Christ would suffer, he thus fulfilled" (Acts 3:18).

We, too, proclaim that Christ has died, that Christ is risen, and that Christ will come again. We rehearse Jesus's first advent as we confess the creeds and sing Advent songs and Christmas hymns. We continue to confess and sing them because our hope is in the Christ who comes to us.

He comes in his word read and preached. He comes in his absolution declared. He comes in his sacraments administered. He who comes to us, comes for us, to forgive our sins and grant us eternal life.

Heavenly Father, your Son's advent fulfilled your promise made to Adam and Eve to bring sinners eternal life. Send your Holy Spirit to refresh us with the gifts given in Word and Sacrament as your Son continues to come to us with the forgiveness of sins, life, and salvation. Amen.

FOR FURTHER REFLECTION, READ MARK 11:1-10.

O Bread of Life from Bethlehem

I AM THE BREAD OF LIFE.

—*John 6:48*

The little town claimed the birthplace of the slayer of giants, the paramount psalmist, and the very man after God's own heart, the shepherd-king. Located about five miles southwest of Jerusalem, Bethlehem's landscape was painted with flowing fields of barley. The house of bread, as is Bethlehem's translation, was the breadbasket of the region.

Now under the occupying rule of the Roman government, Mary and Joseph travel back to David's hometown. They're not here to sightsee or reminisce about the golden days of this small town; they're here because the Romans are putting a census on the books to prepare for an upcoming tax season.

The Gospel writer Luke goes on to tell us that, while they were in Bethlehem, the time came for Mary to give birth (Luke 2:6). In the City of David, another king was to be born, as the prophet Micah foretold, "But you, O Bethlehem Ephrathah, who are too little to be among the clans of Judah, from you shall come forth for me one who is to be ruler in Israel, whose coming forth is from of old, from ancient days" (Mic. 5:2).

Luke continues, "And she gave birth to her firstborn son and wrapped him in swaddling cloths and laid him in a manger, because there was no place for them in the inn" (Luke 2:7). The King of Kings and Lord of Lords is born and placed to rest, not in a comfortable cradle, but where animals look for food.

Fast forward about 30 years. Jesus is teaching and making some bold and unusual statements about himself. Jesus claims, "I am the bread of life" (John 6:48). In the same discourse, he goes on to explain, "I am the living bread that came down from heaven. If anyone eats of this bread, he will live forever. And the bread that I will give for the life of the world is my flesh" (John 6:51).

As we go back to where we started and ponder this season how Jesus, our incarnate Lord, was born of Mary in the town of Bethlehem, we hear these words of Jesus echo in the backdrop of this nativity scene. Jesus, the bread of life, is born in the house of bread and placed to rest in a food trough.

Today, we don't go looking for Jesus in the manger; we go to his Supper where he has promised to be for us. We find Christ in the ordinary bread and wine laid in the mangers of our mouths in which he has pledged to give us his body and blood for us for the forgiveness of sins.

Heavenly Father, continue to feed us with Jesus, our living bread, that we may have life in him and serve you in thanksgiving in everlasting life. Amen.

FOR FURTHER REFLECTION, READ LUKE 2:1-7.

The Messiah, Our Immanuel

ALL THIS TOOK PLACE TO FULFILL WHAT THE LORD HAD SPOKEN BY THE PROPHET: "BEHOLD, THE VIRGIN SHALL CONCEIVE AND BEAR A SON, AND THEY SHALL CALL HIS NAME IMMANUEL" (WHICH MEANS GOD WITH US).

—Matthew 1:22-23

The melodic sermon of Handel's *Messiah* often resonates from the walls of concert halls throughout the world this time of year. Written in 24 days, many regard it as a classic choral and orchestral masterpiece.[7]

The Messiah consists of three parts. The second and third parts consist of meditations on the passion, death, and resurrection of our Lord. The famous "Hallelujah Chorus" often performed for the festival of Easter is included in this section. The first part of the piece, however, spotlights the

---

[7] Handel, G. *The Messiah*. New York, NY: G. Schirmer, Inc.

prophecies leading to and the proclamation of the birth of the Messiah or anointed one.

Handel does not put pen to paper with his own creative lyrics. He expertly sifts through the Scriptures, marrying the words of the prophets to melody, trumpeting the gospel of Christ, the Messiah, our God who was born for us.

In the twelfth movement, Handel quotes the prophet Isaiah: "For to us a child is born, to us a son is given; and the government shall be upon his shoulder, and his name shall be called Wonderful Counselor, Mighty God, Everlasting Father, Prince of Peace" (Isa. 9:6). In the eighth movement, Handel quotes Isaiah again: "Behold, the virgin shall conceive and bear a son, and shall call his name Immanuel" (Isa. 7:14). In this first part of Handel's *Messiah*, we hear of the myriad of names by which the prophets make the Messiah known.

The joy of Advent is in the comfort our Messiah brings. The Wonderful Counselor, Mighty God, Everlasting Father, Prince of Peace, is our Immanuel. The symphonic sermon of the prophets overflows with the mystery of the incarnation of Immanuel, and how he must take upon himself our sins, suffer, die, and rise so that we may be united with him.

Our Immanuel is for you always, just as he promised. He is in the waters of Holy Baptism, uniting himself to you. He gives himself to you to eat and drink in the bread and wine of his Supper as he pledges himself for you. The baby born in

Bethlehem is our God with us, who has come for you that you may have life. Hallelujah!

Heavenly Father, may we ever sing the praise of Immanuel. Send your Holy Spirit that, through your Word and sacraments, we may cling tightly to your promises. Amen.

FOR FURTHER REFLECTION, READ ISAIAH 9:1-7.

The Glory of the Lord

AND THE GLORY OF THE LORD SHALL BE REVEALED AND ALL FLESH SHALL SEE IT TOGETHER, FOR THE MOUTH OF THE LORD HAS SPOKEN.

—Isaiah 40:5

Christmas is full of grandeur. From the appearance of the star leading wise men to the baby Jesus, to a host of angels surrounding shepherds and bursting with song, our Lord's birth was not void of heavenly fanfare. All of these majestic events surrounding the birth of Christ were treasured by his mother, Mary (Luke 2:19).

The prophet Isaiah prophesies of the coming Christ— prophecies of these events surrounding the birth of our Lord and everything he would endure for us. The glory of the Lord, however, is detested by the world. When the long-anticipated glory of the Lord is finally revealed, that glory was, as the prophet Isaiah writes, "despised and rejected by men...as one from whom men hide their faces" (Isa. 53:3).

If the glory of the Lord is not in the fanfare of the events surrounding our Lord, what then is the glory of the Lord?

The glory of the Lord is in his working for you. It is in his incarnation. The glory of the Lord is in his baptism, temptation, suffering, death, and resurrection for you. The glory of the Lord is in Christ crucified for our sins that the mouth of the Lord may speak the words, "your sins are forgiven" (Luke 7:48).

The Gospel writer Luke records three of Jesus's parables on lostness. Jesus tells a parable of a lost sheep, a lost coin, and two lost sons, prompted by Pharisees irritated with Jesus's association with sinners. In these parables, Jesus says, "Just so, I tell you, there will be more joy in heaven over one sinner who repents than over ninety-nine righteous persons who need no repentance" (Luke 15:7). The rejoicing the shepherds witnessed from the angels at the birth of Christ is but a glimpse into the joy of all of heaven bursting at its seams as Jesus brings his lost children from death to life.

The glory of the Lord is in Christ's saving you. It is in the gifts of Christ delivered to you. The preaching of Christ crucified for the forgiveness of all your sins, your pastor's words of absolution, the waters of Holy Baptism, and the Lord's Supper.

We sing with the angels, "Glory to God in the highest, and on earth peace among those with whom he is pleased!" (Luke 2:14). The glory of our Lord has been revealed to us in his saving us. It is finished, for the mouth of the Lord has spoken.

Heavenly Father, as we prepare to celebrate the birth of our Savior, remind us that we are at peace with you, and that you are pleased with us because of your word of forgiveness you spoke through your Son. Amen.

FOR FURTHER REFLECTION, READ LUKE 15:11-32.

Who Am I?

[JESUS] SAID TO THEM, "BUT WHO DO YOU SAY THAT I AM?" SIMON PETER REPLIED, "YOU ARE THE CHRIST, THE SON OF THE LIVING GOD."

—Matthew 16:15-16

The world is perpetually verifying our identities. From air travel to unlocking our phones and checking the boxes that contain a street sign to prove we are not robots, we are proving we are who we say we are on a daily basis.

As Jesus traveled and taught, there were rumors spreading about his identity. Everyone had their own opinion. Jesus posed the question to his disciples, "Who do people say that the Son of Man is?" (Matt. 16:13). The disciples responded with the talk of the town: "Some say John the Baptist, others say Elijah, and others Jeremiah or one of the prophets" (Matt. 16:14). There was no doubt in anyone's mind that Jesus was not an ordinary man. He was sent from God. But for many, it was unclear what that meant.

He certainly didn't have an outward appearance to identify his heavenly status. The baby born in Bethlehem and lauded by angels was now grown and had chosen for himself a band of misfits—fishermen, tax collectors, and the lowly of society—with whom to associate.

To them, Jesus asks the question, "But who do you say that I am?" (Matt. 16:15). Peter wastes no time in waiting for one of his comrades to jump in with their own opinion; he is convinced, "You are the Christ, the Son of the living God" (Matt. 16:16).

Peter's bold confession, however, would soon waver and fall. He would deny Jesus, the Christ, the Son of the living God whom he confessed. Three times in the face of his Lord's death, he denied even knowing Jesus. But despite Peter's denial, Jesus, the one whom he confessed, would never falter.

Jesus, the one in whom our faith and confession is founded, is the solid rock on which our hope is built. While the world unceasingly demands we prove our identity, Jesus gifts our identity to us. Our identity of sinner is deleted from the registrar of heaven, and the identity of saint is written in its place by the blood of the Lamb.

Jesus will never fail us. Jesus gives us his name in the waters of Holy Baptism, and with that comes all of his work for us. To give us his name is to give us his identity. Beloved of the Father and heir of everlasting life.

The world may identify you in a multitude of measurements. Ask the Lord who you are, and he will reply: forgiven, child of God, baptized, redeemed, beloved, and saint.

Heavenly Father, remind us of who you say we are—your redeemed and beloved saints. When we would despair, remind us that we are baptized into your name and belong to you. Amen.

FOR FURTHER REFLECTION, READ JOHN 21:15-25.

Our Fortress in Zion

THEREFORE THUS SAYS THE LORD GOD,
"BEHOLD, I AM THE ONE WHO HAS LAID AS
A FOUNDATION IN ZION, A STONE, A TESTED
STONE, A PRECIOUS CORNERSTONE, OF A SURE
FOUNDATION."

—Isaiah 28:16

He was a wanted man. For now, he was safe within its walls, as the pounding rain and wind battered the landscape. As he was cradled in the protection of a castle, Martin Luther continued his diligent work in translation.

Words became both his constant companion and his haunting foe. The work was grueling as he struggled to find the words in the German language in which he could most faithfully translate the living Word of God from Greek to the language of his people.

This precious book Luther toils over is what has brought him to this castle. What was regarded as only for the academic elites and the priests of the day, Luther was laboring to reform. Within the walls of Wartburg, he translated the New Testament. He translated the Gospels and the accounts of the birth of Christ, which tell of a God who came, not just for the rich, the social elites, and religious leaders, but for the lowly and forgotten.

The God he perceived to be a demanding God, quick to anger, and stringent on mercy was a figment of his Old Adam's making. But now, just as Jesus calmed the rushing waves and whipping wind on the sea of Galilee, his conscience was calmed by the words of Jesus: "For God did not send his Son into the world to condemn the world, but in order that the world might be saved through him" (John 3:17).

The words of the prophets reverberate throughout the Gospel accounts of Christ's birth. The baby is born just as the prophets had foretold. The Lord has laid a sure foundation in Zion, a cornerstone that is Christ, just as Isaiah had said.

Christ the Lord is born to you that you might seek refuge in him. You are bound up and protected in Christ from the accusations of the devil. In Christ, you have been given his righteousness and he, your sin. In the fortress of Christ the Lord, you are forever protected in the peace of sins forgiven.

Heavenly Father, when we are overcome with our sin, protect us in the fortress of your Son's work for us. Guard and keep us that we may be brought to everlasting life in the hope of the sure foundation Christ has built, that in his death and resurrection, we too will live. Amen.

FOR FURTHER REFLECTION, READ PSALM 46:1-11.

Do Not Fear

BUT AS HE CONSIDERED THESE THINGS, BEHOLD, AN ANGEL OF THE LORD APPEARED TO HIM IN A DREAM, SAYING, "JOSEPH, SON OF DAVID, DO NOT FEAR TO TAKE MARY AS YOUR WIFE, FOR THAT WHICH IS CONCEIVED IN HER IS FROM THE HOLY SPIRIT."

—Matthew 1:20

"Do not fear." These are the words of the Lord's angel to Joseph. He and Mary both had reason to fear. By all appearances, Mary and her pregnancy were anything but blessed, as her relative Elizabeth so joyously proclaimed (Luke 1:42). It seemed like a sin against the highest social order. What would people think? Who would believe Mary's story? Would Joseph believe it?

At first, he didn't. He resolved to divorce her, though as quietly as possible so the real father could come to claim the child and marry Mary. The child's real father came to Joseph; God, the Father almighty, creator of heaven and earth, sent a messenger with a message: "Do not fear."

This message is for us too. Except our sinful thoughts, words, and deeds are more than mere appearances. They are all too real. We experience their concrete effects. No matter how well we hide them from our neighbors, they cannot be hidden from the all-knowing, almighty God.

Joseph received a reason to calm his fears. The angel told him, "Do not fear, for the child that Mary carries, the son who is coming, is from God." Despite appearances, there was no sin here in the incarnation, but a blessing—a child by whom all people would be blessed. God was coming to his people, incarnate in the flesh and blood of humanity.

But, for God, the righteous one, to live among us, the unrighteous, is reason to fear. Like Adam and Eve in the garden, we would rather hide than stand in the presence of the God whose commands we break (Gen. 3:8).

But the angel offers further reason for why Joseph need not fear. "Do not fear; for the child that Mary carries, the Son of God, comes to save you from your sins." This is truly good news! The Son of God was sent to rescue, redeem, and save us, not to punish, condemn, or destroy us. Jesus's name means "the Lord saves." His name tells us his mission.

Jesus came to save us from our sins by forgiving them. He paid for our sins by dying on the cross, and he rose from the dead to give us life. This is good news and a good reason to heed the angel's words, "Do not fear."

Heavenly Father, you sent your messenger to Joseph to calm his fears and bring the good news of the Savior. Calm our fears as we listen to the messengers you send to us as they deliver your good gifts to us in word and sacrament. Amen.

FOR FURTHER REFLECTION, READ MATTHEW 1:18-25.

The TWELVE DAYS *of*
CHRISTMAS

Behold, the Lamb of God

AND THE WORD BECAME FLESH AND DWELT AMONG US.

—John 1:14

If you blink, you might miss it. While Luke tells the Christmas story in detail and Matthew gives a chapter-length mention of the details of Christ's birth, John describes this mysterious event in one short phrase: "And the Word became flesh and dwelt among us" (John 1:14).

Many mysterious things surround Christ's birth—the appearance of multitudes of angels, a miraculous star, and a virgin birth, just to name a few. So, why is John not bursting at the seams to retell these wondrous events?

He seems to quickly pass over the beginning of the story. John appears as if he is failing to mention the majestic happenings surrounding that first Christmas day. Or is he?

While many of the other Gospel writers begin with Christ's birth on earth, John goes back even further. Further than the angel's visit to Mary, further even than when he was first promised in the garden. "In the beginning was the Word, and the Word was with God, and the Word was God... All things were made through him, and without him was not anything made that was made" (John 1:1, 3). This child is, as the Nicene Creed states, "very God of very God... by whom all things were created."

John tells us that this Word that came out of the mouth of God, by whom all things were created, has become incarnate and come down to dwell with us. The Word that creates, the Word that speaks "thou shall" and "thou shall not" has chosen to live among us. This baby in the manger is God, the God against whom we have transgressed.

So, why do we celebrate on Christmas Day instead of cowering in fear? Why is this day joyful and not cause for sorrow?

In the very same chapter, John continues by recording the words of John the Baptizer, "Behold, the Lamb of God, who takes away the sin of the world!" (John 1:29). The Apostle John does not waste any time waiting to tell us exactly what this baby came to do. The Word of God has come, not to scold or punish us; he has come to take the punishment we deserve. He has come to live with us that he may redeem us to live with him in glory for eternity. The Word became flesh to take our sins and deal with them in his death on our behalf.

Merry Christmas! The Word has become flesh so that you may not be called "sinner," but "beloved spotless child of God." That is worthy of celebrating.

Heavenly Father, you sent your Son to take our sins away and make us your children. Continue to dwell with us through the working of the Holy Spirit in the hearing of the Word who was made flesh for us, and through the receiving of the holy sacraments. Amen.

> **FOR FURTHER REFLECTION, READ JOHN 1:1-18.**

Echoes of
the Cross

AND FALLING TO HIS KNEES, [STEPHEN]
CRIED OUT WITH A LOUD VOICE, "LORD,
DO NOT HOLD THIS SIN AGAINST THEM."
AND WHEN HE HAD SAID THIS,
HE FELL ASLEEP.

—Acts 7:60

Yesterday, we celebrated the glorious coming of God in the flesh. Today, December 26th, the church celebrates the martyrdom of Stephen—stoned to death for his faithful witness of the gospel.

That these two days share a fence on the church calendar creates an uneasiness to which the spirit of the Christmas holiday beckons us to give a wide berth. But Danish playwright and pastor Kaj Munk, who became a martyr at the hands of the Nazis, observed in a sermon, "Apparently there is a most glaring contrast between the Christmas gospel and that for St. Stephen's Day—between the Christ child and the first Christian martyr. But in reality, there is the closest connection."[8]

Like Jesus, Stephen is put on trial by a jealous opposition. The same Sanhedrin, the same chief priests and elders that judged Jesus, now judge Stephen. Both trials call upon false witnesses. Both defendants testify to the arrival of the Son of Man, the Christ, and to the glory of God accompanying him. Both are innocent. Both are found guilty and sentenced to death.

Stephen's dying prayer also echoes Jesus's words from the cross. Jesus answered, "It is finished," because he came to die for Stephen's stoners and their stiff-necked unbelief.

And who was standing among them, but Saul, the first great persecutor of the church. Better known as Paul, he later received the forgiveness for which Stephen prayed. He proclaimed this forgiveness freely given on account of Christ to the gentiles, to us!

Once we were God's enemies, stiff-necked sinners who rejected him, whose sin killed him. But Christ came to die and rise again. He came to forgive us without measure or payment.

---

[8] Munk, Kaj. *Four Sermons*. Translated by John M. Jensen. Blair, Nebraska: Lutheran Pub. House, 1944, 20.

Heavenly Father, on this day we remember Stephen, the first Christian martyr. Forgive those who seek our harm. And when our last hour comes, graciously bring us to you in heaven with all the saints singing praise to Christ around his heavenly throne. Amen.

FOR FURTHER REFLECTION, READ ACTS 6:1-8:3.

Our Righteous Advocate

MY LITTLE CHILDREN, I AM WRITING THESE
THINGS TO YOU SO THAT YOU MAY NOT
SIN. BUT IF ANYONE DOES SIN, WE HAVE AN
ADVOCATE WITH THE FATHER, JESUS CHRIST
THE RIGHTEOUS.

—1 John 2:1

By the third day of Christmas, the energy and excitement of celebration give way to exhaustion. Presents have been opened, played with, and put aside. Visiting relatives have made or make ready to make their departure. Perhaps you (and your family) are those visiting relatives. The candy and sweets still seem to flow freely. Our attention begins to turn away from Christmas and toward the approaching New Year.

It's here, in the nebulous of losing track of time, reheating leftovers, and complaints of boredom (even though there are plenty of new things to play with) that we commemorate St. John, the Apostle and Evangelist. He is the only apostle believed to have died a natural death. Though he wasn't martyred for the faith like Stephen, he spent a considerable amount of his ministry in exile.

He writes to a community in crisis. They have received great gifts: forgiveness, life, and salvation. But some among them have left in clouds of controversy. They caused doubts. They preached and taught something other than what John proclaimed "concerning the word of life" (1 John 1:1).

Like John's original hearers, we have doubts about our forgiveness, life, and salvation. If Jesus really came in the flesh to make all things new, how come I, as a new creation in Christ, can't seem to love that really annoying family member I only see once a year? I gave my children everything they asked for and more. Why don't I feel like a good parent? I tried to focus on the real reason for Christmas, but in all the busyness I just didn't seem to get anything out of it.

We do well to feel the conviction of our failures. God's law always accuses us of them. But the Son of God came in the flesh to deliver us from the law's accusations. If we look at our own efforts during the Christmas season, we will never feel enough. We will see our sin.

But John's letter calls us to look upon the one who came at Christmas, Jesus Christ, the righteous. He is our advocate, whether or not we feel forgiven or like children of God. Whether or not we feel like we "got anything out of Christmas," Jesus speaks to the Father on our behalf. And, the judgment is final. We are forgiven.

Heavenly Father, when we sin, turn us again to your advocate, Jesus Christ, the righteous one, who was incarnate for us, died and rose again for us, and lives eternally for us. Amen.

FOR FURTHER REFLECTION, READ 1 JOHN 1:1-2:2.

Light in the Darkness

THE LIGHT SHINES IN THE DARKNESS, AND THE DARKNESS HAS NOT OVERCOME IT.

—John 1:5

The light shines in the darkness, the apostle John writes. This is the joy of Christmas. Jesus, our light, has come. But on this day the church recognizes the depths of the darkness of our world into which the light of the world was born.

King Herod was not overjoyed to have the King of the Jews, the promised Messiah born in his neighborhood. After being warned in a dream to leave, Joseph takes Mary and baby Jesus to Egypt. Meanwhile, the darkness of Herod's plot to ensure he remains the one and only king unfolds.

Herod does not politely knock on doors and seek out Jesus's parents to respectfully sort the matter out. He horrifically follows in the footsteps of Pharaoh and has all of the male children in Bethlehem and the surrounding area under two years of age put to death.

Jesus, though safe in Egypt, was not distant from the darkness. Though escaping Herod's plot to take his life, Jesus now resided in the land in which Israel had been bound in captivity. The land Jesus now lodged in was once filled with the death of his people. The cries of Bethlehem echoed the ancient cries of his people in Egypt. The world was filled with darkness.

Though the apostle refers to Jesus as the Light of the World, Jesus was well acquainted with the darkness. The prophet Isaiah describes Jesus as "a man of sorrows and acquainted with grief" (Isa. 53:3).

The Light of the World exchanged himself for our darkness. The apostle Paul writes, "For our sake he made him to be sin who knew no sin, so that in him we might become the righteousness of God" (2 Cor. 5:21). The Light of the World overcame the darkness of sin by taking the darkness of our sin into himself and dying our death.

Jesus is not far off from our darkness; he comes into our darkness that he may bring light, comfort, the forgiveness of sins, and everlasting life. The light shines in the darkness and the day is coming soon when, as the apostle John writes, he will wipe away every tear from our eyes and death shall be no more (Rev. 21:4).

Heavenly Father, you sent your Son into our darkness that through him we may have light. Send your Holy Spirit to comfort us with the hope of everlasting life you have promised to us in the death and resurrection of your Son. Amen.

FOR FURTHER REFLECTION, READ MATTHEW 2:13-18.

Looking for Jesus in All the Wrong Places

AND HE SAID TO THEM, "WHY WERE YOU LOOKING FOR ME? DID YOU NOT KNOW THAT I MUST BE IN MY FATHER'S HOUSE?"

—Luke 2:49

If you've ever searched for something important, you know how your mind races through all the possibilities of what could have happened to it. No doubt, this happened to Mary and Joseph as they anxiously searched for 12-year-old Jesus after they realized he was missing (Luke 2:40-52).

This was the Son of God, the promised Savior of the world. The Son whose miraculous birth from Mary's virgin womb was attested to by angels and praised by shepherds. The Son entrusted to them, whom wise men traveled great distances to worship, and whom Herod sought to kill.

Mary and Joseph looked frantically among the crowded, narrow streets. They retraced their steps. They looked in the places they remembered seeing him last. But they couldn't seem to find him. Why? They were looking in all the wrong places.

In the same way, we look for Jesus in all the wrong places. We search for him in our feelings and intuitions, in abstract spirituality, in the strength of Christian influence on society, in acts of social justice, in nature, and in being a better person. These places are not bad in and of themselves; some of them are quite good. But the question is this: has God promised to be in those places for us?

In the earliest recorded words of his life (Luke 2:49), Jesus makes a powerful statement about who he is, what he came to do, and where he can be found. In those days, for a son to be in his father's house meant he was doing his father's business. Jesus is not just there to be in his Father's house but to carry out his Father's will.

This story foreshadows what would take place 21 years later when Jesus would return to Jerusalem. Once again he would carry out his Father's will—this time by suffering and dying on the cross for the forgiveness of our sins and rising from the dead after three days to bring us new life in him.

Where our sins are forgiven, there Jesus is found. He has promised to be in plain words and water, in simple bread and wine.

There he is found for the forgiveness of our sins and with that forgiveness come life and salvation.

Heavenly Father, just as you sought out Adam and Eve in the garden, you have sent your Son to seek us out while we were yet sinners. Forgive us for looking inward instead of looking to where you promised to be for us. Amen.

> **FOR FURTHER REFLECTION, READ LUKE 2:40-52.**

The Prince of Peace

THEN [JESUS] SAID TO THOMAS, "PUT YOUR
FINGER HERE, AND SEE MY HANDS; AND PUT
OUT YOUR HAND, AND PLACE IT IN MY SIDE. DO
NOT DISBELIEVE, BUT BELIEVE."

—John 20:27

For once, it wasn't Peter. It was Thomas who opened his mouth this time to make a brazen announcement to his fellow disciples: "Let us also go, that we may die with him" (John 11:16). Thomas's enthusiasm and confidence in his Lord shined bright as they made their journey to Bethany.

Now, his passion for his Lord had been all but snuffed out. It had been a long two weeks. Instead of gleaming with the joy of the Passover celebration, he now found himself locked in a room out of fear. "We have seen the Lord," his comrades told him. But his morale was crushed, and he had seen too much to blindly believe that his beloved Lord who was crucified, dead, and buried was alive again.

His hesitation to believe was warranted; after all, who just shakes off the shackles of death and steps out of their grave as if they owned the place?

No one could convince him. The women who visited the empty tomb were not enough to shake his doubt. His comrades' tales of how the risen Jesus had suddenly appeared to them in a locked room were not good enough to break his apprehension. It was too good and, frankly, unbelievable to be true. Unless he saw the marks of the nails in Jesus's hand, unless he could touch his Lord's nail-scarred hands, he would not believe.

> **Eight days later, his disciples were inside again, and Thomas was with them. Although the doors were locked, Jesus came and stood among them and said, "Peace be with you." Then he said to Thomas, "Put your finger here, and see my hands; and put out your hand and place it in my side. Do not disbelieve, but believe (JoÝ 20:26-27).**

It was for Thomas's sake that Jesus was born. It was for Thomas that he died. The Prince of Peace now lives that he may comfort Thomas and strengthen his faith.

It was for you that Jesus was born. It was for you that he died, and it is for your justification that he was raised. The Prince of Peace lives that he may comfort you with the forgiveness of all your sins and grant you peace.

We cannot yet see with our eyes. But we hear with the ears of faith the words of our Lord on the lips of our pastors in the absolution, "peace be with you." We cannot touch the nail marks, but feel the water splashed upon us in Holy Baptism. We receive our Lord's very body and blood in the Lord's Supper as the Prince of Peace strengthens our faith and bids us to not disbelieve, but believe.

Heavenly Father, we thank and praise you for the saving work of your Son. Send your Holy Spirit to comfort us in our weakness and doubting. Amen.

FOR FURTHER REFLECTION, READ JOHN 20:24-31.

Absolution over Resolution

THIS MONTH SHALL BE FOR YOU THE BEGINNING OF THE MONTHS. IT SHALL BE THE FIRST MONTH OF THE YEAR FOR YOU.

—Exodus 12:2

As a new year approaches, we add up our bad habits, criticisms, and haunting mistakes and balance them against our good choices, praises, and achievements. When our ledgers invariably skew red, we resolve to fix them. But our resolutions and any hope of redemption fail because we build them upon a precarious foundation: ourselves. Yet, God gave his people a way to commemorate a new year far different from our new year's resolutions.

Before the final plague against the Egyptians, God came to Moses and Aaron to establish a new-year celebration for his people. It didn't celebrate their worthiness or commemorate how well they worshiped God amid suffering. It celebrated God's work of salvation on their behalf, their absolution as God's judgment passed over them.

"And when your children say to you, 'What do you mean by this service?' you will say, 'It is the sacrifice of the Lord's Passover, for he passed over the houses of the people of Israel in Egypt, when he struck the Egyptians but spared our houses'" (Ex. 12:26-27).

During his last supper, Jesus transformed this Passover meal into a new-year celebration for the absolution of *all* people. Like the original Passover feast, this meal's foundation excludes the work and worthiness of those who celebrate it. Both have a spotless lamb who dies for those partaking in the meal. But one is the fulfillment of the other.

Jesus, our true spotless lamb, instituted this transformed new-year celebration upon *his* work of forgiveness, life, and salvation on the cross. "Take, eat; this is my body... Drink of it, all of you, for this is my blood of the covenant, which is poured out for many for the forgiveness of sins" (Matt. 26:26-28).

Christ's work affects the change our resolutions fail to achieve. We cannot free ourselves any more than the dead can bring themselves back to life. Christ provided forgiveness of our sins by his work—an absolution of our failures, past, present, and future.

God's new year doesn't call for better resolve; rather, it declares us absolved. It doesn't call us to set greater goals than last year, spiritual or otherwise. God's new year speaks grace and mercy. God's new year calls us to see what God has done *for us.*

Our new year says, "do more; be better; make a change." God's new year says, "I rescued you out of slavery to sin because you could not free yourselves. You were dead and I made you alive in me. Take heart, my child; your sins are forgiven. It is finished."

Heavenly Father, we thank you for the gifts you give us in the feast of the Sacrament of the Altar. Send your Holy Spirit to work in us that we may look to your Son for forgiveness, life, and salvation, and work for the good of our neighbor as we trust your promise.
Amen.

FOR FURTHER REFLECTION, READ MATTHEW 26:17-29.

Every Day Is New Year's Day

AND AT THE END OF EIGHT DAYS, WHEN HE WAS CIRCUMCISED, HE WAS CALLED JESUS, THE NAME GIVEN BY THE ANGEL BEFORE HE WAS CONCEIVED IN THE WOMB.

—Luke 2:21

You may have already decided whether or not you were making any New Year's resolutions. That you thought about it at all points to our fallen human desire for fresh starts and second chances. Nothing makes us feel more hopeful or optimistic than the opportunity to take a mulligan in the new year.

January 1st is also a new day in a more profound way: it's the eighth day of Christmas and the commemorative festival day of the naming and circumcision of Jesus. Luke is the only Gospel writer to record Jesus's circumcision and, by doing so, he teaches that Jesus's death and resurrection bring us into a new unending day.

Paul links circumcision to baptism. But he makes it clear that baptism does not replace circumcision as a new law to fulfill. Instead, baptism supersedes circumcision as the gospel fulfilled for us. Paul writes, "In him also you were circumcised with a circumcision made without hands, by putting off the body of the flesh, by the circumcision of Christ, having been buried with him in baptism, in which you were also raised with him through faith in the powerful working of God, who raised him from the dead" (Col. 2:11–12).

Circumcision was given to symbolize the removal of sin from the body. Christ came to bear our sins in his body that he might remove our sin for all eternity.

Circumcision incorporated one into the people of God, connecting one's identity to him who rescued his people from slavery in Egypt. Our baptism incorporates us into the family of God, uniting us to Jesus's death and resurrection. Baptism brings us into a new, unending day. A day in which the devil's power is forever extinguished. A day in which we dwell forever with God, unimpeded by sin. A day in which resurrection reigns and death is no more.

In Christ, every day is a new year's day because he died and was raised for us in order to usher us into a day that has no end.

This day never ends because, like circumcision, the benefits of baptism cannot be undone. Christ's work for us cannot be unfinished. His death, resurrection, and righteousness are unchanging. And they are ours.

Heavenly Father, in Holy Baptism you have united us to your Son. Through baptism, our salvation is finished and you promised to raise us just as Christ was raised for us. Send your Holy Spirit this new year to remind us that, though we may fail, your promise of forgiveness can never be undone. Amen.

FOR FURTHER REFLECTION, READ LUKE 2:21-24.

The Enfleshed Attribute of God

THESE ARE WRITTEN SO THAT YOU MAY
BELIEVE THAT JESUS IS THE CHRIST, THE SON
OF GOD, AND THAT BY BELIEVING YOU MAY
HAVE LIFE IN HIS NAME.

—John 20:31

Theologians have filled libraries with books examining the attributes of God. God is all-powerful as he is the creator of all things. However, if God is all-powerful, he may do as he wills. And, for those who have sinned against such a God, this is a frightening thought.

The book of Proverbs tells us that "the eyes of the Lord are in every place, keeping watch on the evil and the good" (Prov. 15:3). In other words, he does the hard work of Santa, making a list to find out who is naughty and nice.

As if that weren't enough, the apostle John informs us that "God is greater than our heart, and he knows everything"

(1 John 3:20). God doesn't just watch over us; he intimately knows our thoughts. We cannot hide from God.

While these characteristics of God are certainly founded in Scripture, they bring us no comfort in and of themselves. If not in these attributes of our God, where then are we to find comfort?

There is another attribute of God, one that brings comfort: he is embodied in flesh. The incarnate Word, the "image of the invisible God" (Col. 1:15), is the manifested mercy of God.

While theologians spill ink discussing the philosophical traits of God, a theologian of the cross holds onto, clings to the comfort of Christ God enfleshed on the cross. His mercy materialized in Christ crucified for us. The all-powerful, all-knowing, ever-present God wills to be known in the second person of the Trinity, in the incarnate Christ.

The apostle John, in his Gospel account, gives us his thesis statement in the twentieth chapter. John writes, "These are written so that you may believe that Jesus is the Christ, the Son of God, and that by believing you may have life in his name" (John 20:31). The apostle John does not write that we may be frightened of God but be comforted in his Son.

As theologians continue to debate who God is, we can be comforted in this: the God who speaks worlds into existence makes himself known to us that he might save us. The all-powerful God wills us to be saved by his Son.

This baby in a manger is God's word delivered in the flesh. It is a word not of condemnation or of fear, but of comfort in the forgiveness of our sins.

Heavenly Father, comfort us with your gospel; that you did not send your Son into the world to condemn it, but that we may be saved through him. Amen.

FOR FURTHER REFLECTION, READ JOHN 1:1-18.

More in Christ than Was Lost in Adam

FOR IN HIM ALL THE FULLNESS OF GOD WAS
PLEASED TO DWELL

—*Colossians 1:19*

Johann Gerhard composed a remarkable sentence on the incarnation of the Son of God and what it means for us: "We receive more in Christ than we lost in Adam."[9]

We once possessed perfection. We had God's definition of good and not good. We lived with him free of barriers. Of course, all that changed. But the Son of God became incarnate to fix what we broke. He took on flesh so we could once again live a barrier-free existence with the creator and sustainer of all things.

---

[9] Gerhard, Johann, Wade R. Johnston, and Gaylin R. Schmeling. *Sacred Meditations*. Saginaw, MI: Magdeburg Press, 2011.

But Gerhard's words say more. While the Son of God came to restore the righteousness we had lost and to reconcile us with God, we receive even more than that. More than if we remained perfect. More than had we never fallen. In Christ, we receive a God who is not just with us, but one of us.

By the Son's incarnation, we receive a God who shared in our needs, joys, and sufferings. He learned to walk and to work. He smelled. He bathed. He both stopped the wind and broke wind. He slept and wept. He sought solitude and relationship—to love and be loved. He laughed. He conversed. He shared experiences with friends. He celebrated. He felt compassion for the hurting. He felt sadness in loss, the sting of rejection, and the bite of betrayal. He felt breathless as he slowly suffocated; dizzy from losing blood from his wounds; weak from a tortured body, ripped and torn flesh on his back.

The incarnate Christ shared in our suffering in a way more painful than we could fathom. He suffered the greatest injustice as the innocent one condemned to die in place of the guilty. He felt the weight of the world's sin and guilt, of our sin and guilt, as he hung on the cross.

God created humanity in his image. Then he inhabited *that* image. Not just for 33 years, but for eternity thereafter. Jesus did not shed his humanity as he ascended into heaven. He kept it. Christ took on the flesh and blood of humanity and then took that flesh and blood to the throne of God. As the lamb who was slaughtered to purchase us with his blood, he alone is worthy to sit upon it. There he reigns, not only as the image of the invisible God, but as the image-bearer of redeemed and restored humanity, now and forevermore.

Heavenly Father, we daily sin against you, and yet you see us as spotless and righteous on account of your Son. Graciously keep us in the faith until we join with the heavenly saints around the throne singing the praise of the Lamb who was slain for us. Amen.

FOR FURTHER REFLECTION, READ COLOSSIANS 1:15-22.

The Anointed One

AND GOING INTO THE HOUSE THEY SAW THE CHILD WITH MARY, HIS MOTHER, AND THEY FELL DOWN AND WORSHIPED HIM. THEN, OPENING THEIR TREASURES, THEY OFFERED HIM GIFTS, GOLD AND FRANKINCENSE AND MYRRH.

—Matthew 2:11

It was only a week ago when Jesus was eating and enjoying the company of his friends at the house of Mary and Martha. And what a celebration it was! Jesus had raised Lazarus from the dead. Mary, overwhelmed with thanksgiving, anointed the feet of Jesus, covering them with an expensive ointment (John 12:3). Like the aroma of incense rising from the temple, her offering of thanksgiving saturated the air.

As Judas questioned her decision, Jesus spoke in defense of her, "Leave her alone, so that she may keep it for the day of my burial" (John 12:7). And now, a week later, Jesus received another anointing of aromatic spices, this time from Nicodemus.

Jesus was the Christ, the Messiah, the anointed one, as Peter boldly proclaimed (Matthew 16:16). But now, the Christ, the Lord of life, their beloved teacher who had raised Lazarus to life was dead. Nicodemus brought myrrh and aloe to prepare his body for burial. Jesus lay lifeless in the tomb as he was anointed with our iniquities and death on the cross.

As the fragrant gift of Mary foretold her Lord's death, so the gift of myrrh presented by the wise men prophesied our Lord's dying for us.

After accomplishing our salvation in his death on the cross, our Lord burst from his tomb still fresh with the fragrant spices prepared for him. As Jesus appears to his disciples who are overjoyed with his resurrection, he instructs them to baptize "in the name of the Father and of the Son and of the Holy Spirit" (Matt. 28:19).

Jesus anoints us in the waters of baptism with his word, with his very name. In baptism, we are anointed as heirs with Christ of eternal life. The Lord bestows all of his good gifts upon us and makes sinners into saints, children of our Heavenly Father.

Heavenly Father, we have sinned against you and do not deserve your mercy. But you have sent your Son that he may take our iniquities and wash us from our sins. Remind us of the gifts you have bestowed on us in the waters of Holy Baptism. When we sin, turn us back to your word that we may see the Lamb of God who takes away our sin. Amen.

FOR FURTHER REFLECTION, READ JOHN 12:1-8.

It's Time to Take Christ Out of Christmas

AND BEHOLD, I AM WITH YOU ALWAYS, TO THE END OF THE AGE.

—Matthew 28:20

A common sight in the days leading up to Christmas are signs that read, "Jesus is the reason for the season." But the quick disappearance of those signs after Christmas betrays the very thing they hope to inspire. The reality is that those signs are always needed, in every season. Our sinful ability to forget about Christ and his work for us doesn't get put away with the Christmas tree. We need a constant reminder that Jesus is the reason in every season.

Christmas celebrates the incarnation of the Son of God, the Word who took on flesh and dwelt among us. But God's dwelling with his people started before Christ's incarnation. It existed from the beginning. God walked with Adam and Eve, with Enoch and Noah. He was with Abraham, Isaac, Jacob, and Joseph. He was with Moses and the Israelites. And so it goes throughout all of Scripture. God continually dwells with his people in the wilderness, in the promised land, and in exile.

In Jesus, God comes to be with his people in the most physical way. But Christ does not stay behind at Christmas. He doesn't get wrapped up and put away with the nativity set. He comes *with us* out of Christmas through the rest of the year. He left the manger, grew up, and set his face toward Jerusalem and the cross.

Just as Jesus left the manger, he would not stay on the cross. He died to take the sin of the world, my sin and your sin, to the grave. And neither did he remain buried in the tomb. He rose, leaving our sin buried and bringing with him new life.

He continually brings this new life to us as he comes to be with us where two or three are gathered in his name. He comes to be with us in the Scriptures, in the life-giving waters of Baptism, and in the bread and wine that brings his sin-forgiving, life-sustaining flesh and blood to us.

After the Christmas season comes the season of Epiphany, and it can feel crammed between the exciting energy of Christmas and the somber focus of Lent that follows it. But, more than a filler, the arrival of Epiphany (on January 6) reminds us that it's time to take Christ out of Christmas. That Jesus is with us until the end of the age.

Heavenly Father, teach us to give you thanks and praise in every season. We give you thanks that your Son did not remain in the manger, as he did not remain in the grave, but rose victoriously for our justification. In every season, continue to give us your good gifts through your Holy Word and sacraments. Amen

FOR FURTHER REFLECTION, READ PSALM 23.

When they saw
the star, they rejoiced
exceedingly
with great joy.

—MATTHEW 2:10

CPSIA information can be obtained
at www.ICGtesting.com
Printed in the USA
BVHW042331250922
647977BV00006B/174